THE
OVERFLOW
PRINCIPLE

The Overflow Principle

Steven P. Thomason

Published by:

 Vibble Books

www.VibbleBooks.com

Scripture quotations marked (NIV) are taken from the HOLY BIBLE, NEW INTERNATIONAL VERSION®. NIV®. Copyright© 1973, 1978,1984 by International Bible Society. Used by permission of Zondervan.

ISBN: 0-9840670-0-0
13-Digit: 978-0-9840670-0-8

Cover Artwork and Interior Illustration: Steven P. Thomason

Printed in the United States of America

Table of Contents

Session 1
Introduction

Getting Started

Whenever you begin a new endeavor – like reading a new study guide or joining a small group -- it's good to stop and ask yourself, "Why am I doing this?" There are hundreds of possible reasons for picking up a book like this. Perhaps you are reading these words for one of the following reasons: a) you have been coerced into a small group study and if you show up at the next meeting and say that you didn't read the lesson, then you'll be in big trouble with the person who invited you (or your spouse) b) you are cynical of this thing that people have labeled "Christianity" and you want to see what this study has to say about "following Jesus," or c) you want to follow Jesus and you hope this study will give you some helpful tools to use in that endeavor. The truth is that you may fall into category d) all of the above. Don't worry, it is not uncommon to experience all of these motivations simultaneously.

Many people are both cynical and curious at the same time, and have been dragged into a group study by a well-intentioned friend. If you are cynical, or hesitant, rest assured, it's OK. You have good reason. The whole package labeled "Christian" that exists in our culture hasn't exactly lived up to its name. A lot of people have done some really bad things in the name of Jesus. That's because the thing called "the church" is full of imperfect people, just like you, who are trying to make sense out of things. They are on a journey of discovery. Some are honestly seeking and growing, while others believe they have "arrived" and are empowered to pass judgment on people. Some are full of genuine love and compassion, others are full of fear and reaction.

The good thing is that growing spiritually doesn't mean you are supposed to follow a church. It doesn't even mean you need to become religious. It's all about discovering God and learning how to grow in a relationship with God. That's what this study will try to help you do.

Before we dive into it, let's set some expectations and a baseline of understanding. This study is built upon some basic assumptions:

First, there is not one definitive process, methodology, set of steps, rules, or disciplines that captures the total picture of spiritual growth and development. This study does not claim to be the final word in spiritual growth, nor does it claim to be the first word. It's simply a word in a long string of words that have come into your life. The process of learning and spiritual formation is simply a long conversation along a journey. Hopefully you'll find this study to be a positive contribution to that conversation.

Secondly, this study is based upon the belief that Jesus is our teacher and the example we follow. If you don't know who Jesus is, then you may want to spend some time reading the first four books of the New Testament – Matthew, Mark, Luke, and John. These are the only documents we have that record the story of his life. If you think you know who Jesus is, be careful. Much of the doctrine that has been passed down to us over 2,000 years has been processed and reprocessed through a myriad of religious, philosophical, political, and cultural filters. It is the mandate of every generation to carefully examine the New Testament records, evaluate them properly within the first-century cultural framework, and then draw the relevant connection to our own culture and the issues at hand in our century. That, however, is the topic of another study. For now, we assert that it is the Jesus of the New Testament that we follow – the Jewish teacher who brought a message of liberation to the poor, sick, outcast, and oppressed people who lived under the Tyranny of the Roman Empire and the Bullying of the Religious Elite.

Third, spiritual growth is a process. It takes time, trial, and error. It is not a quick fix or a 1-2-3, linear process that will lead you to a final destination called Spiritual Maturity. All of the categories that we will explore in this study are not stand alone, sequential steps. Rather, they are likes sections of a choir, or systems in the human body. All the parts need to be present and functioning in harmony in order for the whole to be healthy and productive. The process is like a dance, or like an artist that steps up close to work on the detail of one part of the picture for a while, and then steps back and looks at the whole to make sure everything is in balance. In and out, back and forth, breathing, learning, growing.

Let's begin...

A Fruity Picture

> » **Read John 15:1-17** (the fourth book in the New Testament, chapter 15, verses 1-17)
>
> *What analogy does Jesus make in this passage?*
>
> *What roles do the following characters play in the analogy: The Father, Jesus, the disciples?*
>
> *What is the end goal for the vine, to bear_____?*
>
> *How does the branch accomplish this goal?*
>
> *What happens if the branch does not function this way? Why? What does this mean?*
>
> *What relationship does Jesus have with the disciples? What is your reaction to this?*
>
> *What did Jesus command?*
>
> *In your own words, and according to Jesus' teaching in this passage, what do you need to do to bear fruit?*

The Two Basic Commandments

» **Read Mark 12:28-31**

What are the two simple commands that Jesus told us to follow?

Spend some time thinking and/or writing about what it might look like in your life if you obeyed these commands? Would anything have to change for you to be able to do it? Would anything change as a result of doing it?

It's About Overflow

Congratulations! You made it through your first Bible Study portion of this book. We looked at what Jesus said it meant to be his disciple (the word disciple means *student*: someone who follows a teacher and learns from him). Sounds pretty easy, right? After all, he only gave us two commands to obey, and they both start with Love.

How did you react to these passages? Your reaction may fall into one of the following categories:

Explosion

You may think, "Let's get out there and start loving more." You may have already started your plan for how you are going to work harder at loving God. You are going to go to church more often, pray harder (maybe even get on your knees when you pray), give more money to the church, take notes during the sermon, maybe even join a committee. And then, you are going to work really hard at being nicer to people. You're going to smile. You plan to be nice to the office gossip. Hey, you might even volunteer at the local shelter.

Implosion

Perhaps you reacted differently when you read those commands. Perhaps, instead of deciding to work harder, you decided to give up. You imploded, or at least deflated. You thought, "I can never love God enough, or love my neighbor enough to avoid getting cut off from the vine. I might as well give up."

Regardless of your reaction, here is some advice – slow down, and cheer up. Look again at what Jesus said about the branch. Did he tell the branch to get to work and produce more fruit? No, he didn't. He told the branch to *abide*. Here's where we get to take a deep breath. John 15 was not a threatening passage in which Jesus said, "If you don't obey me and work harder to produce fruit, then God's going to cut you out and throw you away!" That would be pretty scary. Jesus said just the opposite. He said "abide." The word means *live in, stay put, remain, hang out, dwell*. This is a welcoming word. Jesus is saying, "Don't get caught in the performance trap. Don't focus on producing 'good works' or 'fruit.' Instead, focus on your relationship with me. Slow down and hang out in the reality that God loves you and you are safe and secure in my loving arms. If you will relax and let yourself be loved by God, then the love of God will flow into you, like the sap flowing from the vine into the branch, and the love of God will transform you and allow good fruit to flow out of your life, naturally. When you are connected to the vine, you don't have to work hard to produce fruit, it just happens because that is who you are. As soon as you turn away from the restful place of enjoying the love of God and start focusing on working harder at producing fruit, then you have disconnected from the Vine. What happens when a branch disconnects? It stops producing fruit, hardens up, and dries out. What does the gardener do to dried up branches? He cuts them off. Does he do this because he's vengeful or angry? No. He has to, because the branch is dead and worthless. The Father didn't do it to the branch, it was the natural outcome of the branch's focus. You see, either way, it is about natural outcomes. If you remain connected, then fruit grows. If you focus on doing it yourself, then the branch dies. It's that simple."

At this point in the study we will change metaphors and turn from the vine and the branches to a picture of a clay pot and water. Look closely at the following illustration.

At the center of the chart is a simple clay pot. That represents our heart. In 2 Corinthians 4:7 Paul – one of the first teachers after Jesus left -- tells us that we are nothing more than jars of clay. We are made of simple stuff. Yet, the great miracle is that we have the potential to house the infinite mystery of God's glory inside our jars of clay.

In the first command, Jesus said to love God with your heart, mind, soul, and strength. It could be rendered like this: Love God with your whole heart – your mind, spirit, and body. The human being is comprised of three essential components – the Mind, the Spirit, and the Body. In this study we will focus on how we can engage in the love of God with each of these parts.

Notice that there are three streams flowing down through the sections of Mind, Spirit, and Body and into the empty pot. Also notice that the words

above each section read, "Receiving God's Love with my..." You see, the key to Loving God is to realize that we can't really do it on our own. Our job is not to work really hard at loving God, but it is to yield ourselves to God and simply allow his love to flow into us through our mind, spirit, and body.

Reality Check

We need to stop right here and make something clear. One of the biggest reasons that people don't grow spiritually is because they don't believe that God loves them. Somewhere along the way, perhaps through a condemning parent, the disapproval of an authority figure, or a judgmental church, they have picked up the notion that God does not approve of them. Perhaps they have done something in their past they believe God cannot forgive and, therefore, cannot love them.

What about you? Do you believe that God loves you?

Look at the following phrases:

> **For God did not send his Son into the world to condemn the world, but to save the world through him.**
> **- John 3:17 (NIV) -**

> **Therefore, there is now no condemnation for those who are in Christ Jesus,**
> **- Romans 8:1 (NIV)-**

God loves you. God created you. God wants you. God invites you into a loving relationship. Nothing you can do will ever change the love of God. Your greatest enemy is your disbelief. God does not ask you to jump higher, or be better. Jesus simply says, "abide." Come home to the love of God and soak it in.

» **Let's explore this idea through the following passages.**

   Matthew 12:33-37
   Romans 15:13

   What is the source of a person's outward actions?

Here's the bottom line. We can't love others and produce good fruit until we are first filled with the love of God. If we try to produce good fruit on our own, in our own strength, it will be sour and empty. However, if we focus on loving God and being filled with his love, then we will have an infinite supply of good fruit to overflow to anyone who has need.

Cultivating a Romance

The key to developing a strong relationship with God is to simply commit to the relationship, not the ritual. We are called to love God, not perform for him and hope he loves us. If we want to be filled up with God's love and be able to overflow his love to everyone around us then we need to make sure that we understand that this whole Christian thing is about cultivating a relationship with God. Nothing more. If you are authentically, passionately in love with God, then you will naturally begin to resemble God.

In this study we will use the language of a love relationship in order to discuss the Spiritual Disciplines.

You want to develop a relationship with God, right? So, what does it take to cultivate any kind of quality relationship?

First, you need to know about the other person. You need to study that person and learn about who they are, where they come from, what makes them tick, what ticks them off. This kind of learning requires time spent with that person and quality communication back and forth. That is what it means to **love God with your MIND**. You learn about God by spending time listening and finding out who God is.

Second, you need to connect at an emotional level with that person. Try to think about the first time you fell in love. There was a strange feeling in your stomach, your palms got sweaty, and your heart beat a little faster when that person walked in the room. These emotions went beyond information. They were beyond reason. They ignited your spirit and connected you with that person in a way that you were not connected to anyone else. We need to experience that kind of connection with God as well. God is not just an abstract concept to be studied. God is a personality who wants to be the lover of your soul. That is what it means to **love God with your SPIRIT**.

Third, you need to take action with your love. Healthy couples touch each other. They hold hands, they cuddle, they give each other gifts, and they take care of each other's physical needs. Married couples share in physical intimacy. God gave us physical bodies and physical resources so that we can express our love in very concrete, practical ways. We demonstrate our love to God by giving out of our physical resources and by loving others through acts of service and mercy. That is what it means to *love God with your BODY*.

Finally, the overflow of a heart that is falling in love with God is a life that demonstrates love to your neighbor. Who is my neighbor, you may ask? That's simple. Your neighbor is everyone and everything. Think of your relationships like the cascading pots in the illustration, or as concentric circles moving away from you like ripples on water that fan out from a drip of water. The inner circle is your most intimate friend. If you are married, this should be your spouse. The next ring includes your closest friends, with whom you share your true self. Next is your family and friends. After that comes your "faith community." This doesn't necessarily mean a church. This is the larger group of people with whom you identify and associate with...your preferred social network.

Up to this point, the people in these circles are your **Comfortable Neighbors**. It's fairly easy to love these people, because they will generally return your love. When Jesus was asked the question, "who is my neighbor?" He answered with a shocking story. He said that your neighbor is a person who is outside of your comfortable circles of friends. Your neighbor is the person on the other side of the "tracks." The person you don't understand, your **Uncomfortable Neighbor**.

That's right, everyone is your neighbor. God's Love, the Kingdom of God that Jesus brought, is a way of living where we demonstrate authentic love for everyone, even our enemy. It's a place where we are transformed from self-centered, self-protective, fear-based individuals into other-oriented, love-based members of the global community who seek to find mutually beneficial modes of being that allow everyone the opportunity to thrive on this beautiful planet that God has entrusted to us.

Does that sound like the kind of world in which you would like to live? That is the world Jesus envisioned for us. He envisioned it through his teaching, he demonstrated it through his death, he empowered it through his resurrection, and he commissioned it when he left and told us to go out and spread the Good News of this way of being. Teach people how to live like this, get them to saturate themselves in God's love and then overflow it to everyone.

Group Discussion

» **What are some of your expectations for this study and/or group?**

» **What was Jesus trying to communicate with his image of the vine and the branches?**

» **Where are you on the "I believe God Loves Me" scale? Do you strongly believe this, or is this a difficult concept to grasp? Why?**

» **Does the idea of cultivating a "romance" with God seem foreign or natural to you? Why?**

» **Of the five areas highlighted in the Overflow Illustration -- Mind, Spirit, Body, Comfortable Neighbor, Uncomfortable Neighbor -- which one most resonnates with you and which one seems most unfamiliar?**

» **What questions did this study raise in your mind?**

Session 2
Receiving God's Love
with Your Mind

Loving is a Learning Process

Falling in love is a wonderful experience. True, long-lasting love generally does not happen instantly. It is a process. What does a couple do when they first start getting to know each other? They go out on dates. They spend hours sitting in the corner booth of the diner exchanging stories about their childhood, past relationships, favorite movies, etc. Then, when they get home, they spend another two hours on the phone! Why? They spend time talking because they desperately want to know who this new fascinating, captivating person is. They want to soak up as much information as they can about the person so that they can know them in a deeper way.

That is how it is in our relationship with God. We need to soak up as much information about God as we can so that we can know God at deeper and deeper levels.

The question is, "How?" How do we learn about God? One of the best
places to start learning about God is in the Bible. If we want to grow in
our relationship with God, then we need to become students of the Bible,
because this book is the primary means and most universally accepted
manuscript through which the reality of God's personality has been
recorded and communicated throughout the generations.

The Role of the Mind

Before we go further in our discussion about the role of the Bible in our
relationship with God, let us first stop and take a moment to discuss the
role of the mind itself. The mind is the gateway through which our lives
are transformed.

» **Read the following verses.**

Romans 8:5-7
Romans 12:2

What role does the mind have in the transformation process?

Our mind, our will, our volitional choices, are the executive function within
us. Our behaviors are dictated by what we believe to be true. If we believe
a chair is safe to sit on, then we will sit on it without even thinking. If we
do not believe it is safe, we will not sit on it. If we believe God loves us
and wants us to love others, then we will be more likely to overflow love
to others. If we believe that God accuses us, withholds love, and plays
favorites, then we will be more likely to treat others with suspicion and
self-preservation.

Our emotions and our bodies are in, or should be in, submission to our minds. Emotions rise and fall like the tide and, while they are intense, are not always based upon truth. The mind, however, is based upon the careful examination of truth and is able to make decisions based upon thought-out reasoning. When the emotions overpower the mind, then anything can happen, sometimes good, sometimes bad. When the mind has become convicted of truth, and is in its executive function, then it can actually calm the emotions down in even the most adverse circumstances.

It is important for us to remember that being a follower of Jesus in not something that is based upon an emotional experience. Just because we feel, or don't feel, something does not make it true or false. Yes, it is an incredibly emotional experience (we'll talk about that in the study of Spirit), but it is not based on an emotional experience. It is based on truth that is ascertained with the mind, is translated into conviction, that is then sent as directives to the emotions and the body, bringing them into harmony with the mind and the will of God.

Think of the emotions as a wild stallion and the mind as the horse whisperer – the rider who wants to mount the horse. A wild horse is pure energy, but it is dangerous and unproductive. A rider without a horse is stagnant and unproductive as well. Yet, when a rider can bridle the horse and bring its energy into focus, then both rider and horse can reach levels of power and productivity that were not previously possible. Emotions without the bridle of logic are unpredictable and often destructive. Logic without emotion is stale, dead, and often cruel. Together, under the leadership of the Spirit, they are focused energy that can ignite the Kingdom of God.

Simply put, regardless of our personality, we must begin with our mind and learn the basic truths about God in order to be able to ensure that the God that we are experiencing is the one true God and not an imposter that wants to woo us away with a flashy smile, smooth talk, and hyped up emotions.

The Bible is the Key to Loving God with Your Mind

Let's examine what the Bible says about itself and its role in our relationship with God.

» **Read the following verses and answer the questions.**

Psalm 119:9-16
Psalm 119:105-112
Romans 15:4

What attitude does David have for the Word of God in these two passages from Psalms?

What benefit does he feel the Word has for the person who will follow it?

According to all three passages, what is the purpose of scripture (the word "scripture" simply means "something that is written down." In this context it is just a fancy word for the Bible)?

2 Timothy 3:10-17
In this passage, Paul speaks to his student, Timothy, to encourage him to not give up in his role as a spiritual leader in the church. What does he tell Timothy about the role of scripture in his life?

Practical Tools for Loving God with your Mind

Go on a DATE with God

The following is a practical guide to help you get started in spending time with God. Just like the young couple falling in love, you must make a D.A.T.E. with God on a regular basis.

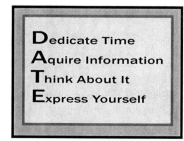

Dedicate Time
Aquire Information
Think About It
Express Yourself

Dedicate Time

In a world that is filled with frenetic activity that can easily consume us, the word *intentionality* is the key to our survival. The only way to do the important things in life is to make time. Every person is allotted exactly the same number of hours in every week. How we use those hours is a matter of priorities and a conscious act of the will.

If you have never spent time with God before, then perhaps you can start by setting aside 15 minutes each day, five days a week, for this DATE. Put in on your calendar. Make no exceptions. It's the most important meeting of your day. Without it there will be no filling, and without filling, there will be no spilling (overflow).

Aquire Information (Read Scripture)

You will not be able to read the entire Bible in one sitting, nor should you do so. Don't be overwhelmed by the size and scope of the book. You know what they say about eating an elephant. How do you eat an elephant? One bite at a time.

The way to understand God through the study of scripture is to simply begin reading. A little bit every day.

When God led his people through the desert in the book of Numbers, he provided daily bread for them called Manna. Jesus said that his word is our daily bread. The Bible is one of the ways that we can hear the word of God. Think of it as a nutritional power pack for each day. In the same way that you would not eat only once a week, so you should not go without scripture for more than a day.

Think About What You've Learned (Meditate)

The word *meditate* conjures up many varied images in our culture today. It is important to make a clear distinction between Eastern meditation and Christian meditation.

Eastern meditation is the process of slowing down one's body and clearing one's mind for the purpose of emptying the mind and being open to anything. Christian meditation is the process of slowing down one's body and clearing the mind of distractions for the purpose of focusing on the Word of God and listening to the Holy Spirit.

There is a big difference between these two disciplines. While some of the external forms of Eastern meditation (breathing and stretching exercises, for example) may be helpful for the Christian, the basic premise of each discipline is diametrically opposed to one another. Eastern philosophy does not believe in an objective God who can be known and, thus, does not believe in the spiritual realities that swirl around us (angels, demons, etc.) Eastern meditation can be dangerous in that it creates a vacant room in the mind that invites any and every influence into it. Christian meditation, on the other hand, believes that God is an objective reality that can be known. Christian meditation blocks out distracting influences, both physical and spiritual, and opens the door to the Holy Spirit and the truth of God's word so that it can be contemplated in peace and serenity.

Here's a simple starter plan for meditation in your DATE.

- ▶ *Find a quiet place for your DATE.*
- ▶ *Begin by taking a few deep breaths and stretching your neck and shoulders.*
- ▶ *Ask God to help you focus and pay attention to what he is going to say to you through your reading.*
- ▶ *Keep a notebook handy to jot down thoughts and ideas that come to you as you read.*
- ▶ *After you have read, take another deep breath and ask God to expose to you any of the following things that may be pertinent to your life as a result of the reading.*

  - ◊ A sin to confess
  - ◊ A prayer to repeat
  - ◊ An attitude to avoid
  - ◊ A command to obey
  - ◊ An example to follow
  - ◊ A Prayer to repeat
  - ◊ An error to avoid
  - ◊ A truth to believe
  - ◊ Something to be thankful for

Express yourself (Pray, Journal, Sing, etc.)

So far on this date you have mostly been listening. Everyone knows that a date in which one person does all the talking and the other person does no talking is one that will not likely lead to a flourishing relationship. Now it is your turn to talk. End your DATE by responding to God. This is commonly called prayer. The word *prayer* can often conjure up some very stuffy and pretentious images in the mind – depending on your past experience. Yet, prayer is simply talking to God. If God has spoken to you then you will likely have something to say in response. Go ahead and say it. God wants to hear from you. A prayer doesn't have to look a certain way; it simply has to be real.

Prayer can take on many forms. You may want to speak out loud to God. You may want to speak within your own thoughts (God knows your thoughts, remember). You may want to write your prayers in a journal. You might want to take a walk and ponder creation. You might want to draw a picture or write a poem. How you express yourself to God is largely determined by who you are. We will discuss prayer and worship more later.

Here are some other ways that you can cultivate your mind and get to know God better.
- ► *Listen to teaching on tape or radio*
- ► *Take classes*
  - ◊ Through local church
  - ◊ Online
  - ◊ Bible College or Seminary

- ► *Memorize passages from the Bible (A Form of Meditation)*

  Memorization itself is an excellent discipline for the old gray matter. Memorizing scripture is a double bonus because it not only stimulates your intellect; it also stores God's living Word in your heart and gives the Holy Spirit an arsenal of truth to work with. Think of memorized scripture as coals in a fire pit. When they are stoked a flame will pop up. The more coals there are, the more potential for fire there is. When you get into a life situation, the Holy Spirit will go to the fire pit of your mind and stoke whatever coals you have placed there in order to create a fire that can respond to your situation. If you don't put any coals in your mind, then there won't be a fire.

» **Now is as good a time as any to commit to a daily DATE with God. Right now, grab your calendar and figure out when it is going to happen. Before the day is over tell someone about your commitment and ask them to hold you accountable to keeping that DATE.**

Group Discussion

» **Tell about a time when you fell in love. What kind of things did you do to get to know the person?**

» **How did you respond to the idea that the mind needs to be in control of the emotions? Is this a true statement? Why?**

» **What role does the Bible play in learning to love God? Why?**

» **What experience do you have with the Bible?**

» **How is Christian Meditation different from Eastern Meditation? How is it the same?**

» **When and how will you make a "DATE" with God this week?**

Session 3
Receiving God's Love
with Your Spirit

An Authentic Experience

In the last lesson we used an analogy that compared human emotions to a wild stallion and the rational mind to a rider with a bridle. If you are an emotion-centered person you may have been somewhat offended by those ideas. If you are a mind-centered person, you were probably feeling pretty smug, thinking, "Yeah, you tell 'em. I'm tired of all those over-emotional types."

In this session we get to turn the tables a little. While it is true that our knowledge of the truth must precede conviction, we must also remember that knowledge without compassion or emotion is completely useless. The rider without a horse is just a guy standing there with a limp piece of leather in his hand. The stallion is the energy. It is the life and the power behind the work that needs to be done. When brought into harmony with the mind and will of God, the Spirit can do amazingly powerful things.

When we talk about loving God with your SPIRIT, we are talking about experiencing the presence of God in a non-rational – better yet, a suprarational – way which defies words. We feel God's presence. We become invigorated by the relationship we have with God. Our step is quickened and our focus is sharpened. When we love God with our Spirit it is as if we get a shot of spiritual adrenaline running through our veins. When our spirit is connected to God, we can move mountains.

> » **Read Psalm 42:7**
> *How does this song writer describe his relationship with God?*

God is spirit and it is the spirit within us that truly connects to God, on God's turf, and breathes life and energy into us.

An Authentic Expression

The question is, "How do I connect to God with my spirit? What does it look like?" This question has historically sparked some volatile discussion in the church. In fact, it has divided the church. Some people say that the only authentic response to the filling of the Holy Spirit is to speak in tongues and/or perform miracles. Others say that the Spirit leads us into quiet places of inward contemplation. Still others say that the only real evidence of the Spirit is manifested through social action.

Perhaps there is an alternate answer that, instead of creating a black and white, either/or solution, will spread out a colorful kaleidoscope that is more in keeping with the nature of God's creative Spirit. Perhaps the way we connect to God with our spirit is determined by our natural personality type.

Here's an example.

Suppose you were able to go to the Superbowl, but you were not really interested in the game. This allowed you the opportunity to observe the people and be emotionally detached from what was going on down on the field. As you sat down you noticed that the two people on either side of you were obviously cheering for the same team.

The guy on your right is decked out in the team colors. As soon as you sat down he reached out his hand to shake yours and started talking. On the opening kickoff he ripped off his shirt and exposed the fact that he had painted his body in the team colors as well. Throughout the entire game he was standing up, screaming, drinking beer, and allowing himself to get caught up in every play of the game.

The guy on your left was quite a different picture. He was dressed very conservatively. However, his pen did display the team logo. He never really made eye contact with you. When the game started he pulled out a pad of paper and began keeping stats on his favorite players. He seemed a bit annoyed by the painted man next to you, but tried to keep his mind on the game.

Very different men, aren't they?

Now, imagine that it has come down to the final seconds of the fourth quarter. The team that these men cheer for is down by two points. They are on the 20 yard line. They line up for a field goal. The crowd holds its breath. The ball is snapped. 3...2...1. The kick is away. Time runs out. FIELDGOAL!!! Victory by one point in the final second!

Now, you look to the right. What does the painted man do? Of course, you can predict that, based on his behavior to this point, he goes absolutely ballistic and starts high-fiving and hugging everyone within a five person radius.

Look at the guy on the left. He bends over, clenches his fist, and whispers a strong, but silent, "Yes!"

Which guy loved his team more? Is it fair to say that the painted man was a better fan because he was flamboyant and extremely expressive about his passion? No. The man on the left was equally passionate, but drastically different in his expression of that passion.

So it is with the worship of God. The HOW we connect with him is greatly determined by the HOW we are wired in our personality.

In the next section we will look at the various, practical ways that people with different personalities can connect with God and experience God authentically.

First, we need to look at one thing that is universal for all followers of Jesus. When we are on a DATE with God, God wants us to talk as well as listen. Like a good husband with his wife, or a good mother with her children, God simply takes pleasure in hearing our voice and seeing that we trust enough to pour out our hearts.

Our Common Expression – Prayer

There are many different types of prayer. All of them are necessary for us to have good, honest, and well-balanced communication with God. The following list describes the different kinds of prayer.

- ▶ **Praise** *(telling God how wonderful and powerful God is)*
- ▶ **Thanksgiving** *(Thanking God for all the ways God has helped us)*
- ▶ **Confession** *(Admitting our sins and failures to God and asking to be forgiven)*
- ▶ **Intercession** *(Praying for other people who are in need of God's strength and help)*
- ▶ **Supplication** *(Asking God to supply our needs)*

» **Read the following verses and identify which type of prayer is being used.**

Psalm 38:18

Hebrews 13:15

Luke 11:3

Ephesians 5:20

James 5:16

» **Jesus taught us how to pray in Matthew 6:9-13.**
In which verses does He talk to God about God?

With what kind of attitude does He speak to God?

In which verses does He speak to God about requests He has?

What kind of attitude does He display in the kinds of requests He makes?

How does this model of prayer affect the way you order your prayers?

» **The Apostle Paul also gave us great examples of prayer. His prayers were prayers of intercession (praying for other people).**

Read Ephesians 3:14-21 and make a list of things that you could pray for people you know.

Take a moment right now and use these requests to pray for someone you know. Write down the name of the persons(s) for whom you prayed.

Perhaps you could create a prayer list? A list can help you remember things you might otherwise forget to pray about. It can include:

▶ *Your family*

▶ *Your friends and acquaintances*

▶ *Your pastor and church*

▶ *Missionaries and Christian workers you know*

▶ *Those who oppose you*

▶ *Governmental authorities*

▶ *Your personal need*

Our Unique Expression

In the Superbowl example we observed that people will respond differently when faced with the same situation. These differences come from our prewired personality types.

Sadly, many Christians can fall into the trap of Spiritual Comparison. One scenario may look like this; a person walks into a public worship gathering, we'll call her Pam. As the music begins Pam notices a woman across the isle that is, very noticeably, getting caught up in the music. This woman begins to shake and to cry, and even to speak in tongues. Pam reflects on the fact that the music did nothing for her and she didn't feel any closer to God than when she started. Pam begins to question whether she really loves God because she did not respond to the music service in the same way that the other woman did.

Pam is a volunteer at the Women's Resource Center. She doesn't counsel people, she simply donates her cleaning services to the facility and helps organize the donations that are brought in. After an afternoon of cleaning and organizing, she steps back and feels very fulfilled that she had done a good job. What she doesn't realize is that her act of service was every bit as much an authentic expression of experiencing God's presence as the weeping woman in the music service.

> »   **Read Colossians 3:17**
>
>   *According to this verse, in what spheres of our life does God desire to penetrate?*

Discover Your Spiritual Pathway

In the book *Sacred Pathways: Discovering Your Soul's Path to God*[1]
Gary Thomas proposes that there are different pathways upon which
individuals can connect to God in a spiritual act of worship. These
pathways are dependant upon the individual's God-given personality.

The following list is a brief description of Thomas' types. Read through
this list and see if any of them sound like your natural tendency toward
interacting and experiencing God.

Naturalists: Experiencing God in Nature

A Naturalist feels God most deeply when away from the noise, pollution,
and chaos of modern civilization. The primal energy of the universe is the
fingerprint of God's spirit that resonnates deeply within the Naturalist.

Sensates: Experiencing God with the Senses

Sensates rely heavily upon the physical senses - sight, sound, touch, taste,
smell -- to relate to God. A tactical worship experience, complete with
liturgy, incense, iconography, and response, is very meaningful.

Traditionalists: Experiencing God through Ritual and Symbol

Traditionalists connect with God through rituals, symbols, sacraments, and
sacrifice. Routine patterns of worship and daily practice bring peace and
comfort. To the traditionalist, God is a God of order that brings peace out
of an normally chaotic world.

Ascetics: Experiencing God through Solitude and Simplicity

Ascetics want to be left alone - with God. The hustle and bustle of people
racing through religious rituals and programs breeds nothing but anxiety.
The ascetic desires freedom from distraction in order to focus completely
on God.

[1]Sacred Pathways (Zondervan: Grand Rapids, 2000)

Activists: Experiencing God through Involvement

Activists see the world through the lens of social justice. They understand that true religion is taking care of the widows and the orphans. Nothing brings them closer to God than when they stand up for justice and see change in society.

Caregivers: Experiencing God by Loving Others

Caregivers understand that they are the hands and feet of Christ. The concept of God can be a detached abstraction and worship services are often empty. For the caregiver, the spirit of God pulses in the most vibrant way when real needs are met in people's lives.

Enthusiasts: Experiencing God with Mystery and Celebration

Excitement and mystery in worship is the spiritual lifeblood of enthusiasts. They are the people who move, clap, cheer, and get caught up in the worship service. They are the cheerleaders that spur the preacher and the worship team on. God is felt in a nearly tangible way when the Spirit moves through the room.

Contemplatives: Experiencing God through Adoration

Contemplatives know God as their lover. Spirituality is a Divine Romance between God -- the groom -- and the church -- the bride. The contemplative enjoys spending time basking in the love of God and meditating on the depth of this relationship.

Intellectuals: Experiencing God with the Mind

Intellectuals study God first as a concept. Through logic and reason, sifted carefully through worldviews and comparative religions, the intellectual comes to terms with the reality of God.

» **Where Are You?**

Which category most resonnated with your experience?

How will you cultivate this pathway in the weeks ahead?

visit **www.vibbleblog.com/spirit** to find more resources regarding loving God with your SPIRIT.

Group Discussion

» **What do you get most excited about in life? Why?**

» **Which fan are you more like in the Superbowl illustration?   How is this demonstrated in your life?**

» **Before this session, what were your ideas about prayer? Has your view changed at all? Why?**

» **Which Spiritual Pathway most resonnated with you? Why?**

» **How will you explore ways to cultivate this pathway in the future?**

Session 4
Receiving God's Love with Your Body

The Physical Reality of Love

We have physical bodies in a real, physical world. With these physcial bodies we interact with everything around us. Without bodies we would not be able to express love for another person. We wouldn't be able to speak kind words, smell their sweet perfume, look deeply into their eyes, listen to their voice, or feel the warmth of their body cuddled close to ours. Because of the physical body, we can express concrete acts of love to another person.

These expressions of love intensify as the relationship goes deeper into the inner sanctum of our heart. The person on the outer ring of acquaintance we greet with a friendly smile and a handshake. Familiar friends we will hug with a warm embrace. For the person in our family we hold hands, rub shoulders, cuddle on the couch. And then, for the person with the deepest relationship, the spouse who has been bonded to us through the life-long commitment of marriage, we express love through the ultimate convergence of mind, spirit, and body and bond through the love that is designed to produce life itself and bear children.

Throughout history and across religious traditions — both east and west — there has been a perennial conflict between the spiritual and the physical, the immaterial and the material, the sacred and the secular. This conflict has led some to deny the existence of the spiritual altogether and claim that the universe is nothing more than matter. It has led others to go the opposite direction and claim that the physical universe is simply an illusion and everything is pure mental energy. Still others claim that there is a division between the spiritual, which is good, and the physical, which is evil.

This perceived conflict is unfortunate. The mind, spirit, and body are intertwined and inseparable.

» **Read Genesis 1:26-31**

What is God's attitude toward the physical world?

God created the physcial universe and called it good. God created the physical pleasures of eating, drinking, hard work, art, music, and love. They are a gift to us so that we may engage in the other-oriented love that is the very essence of the divine.

» **Read 1 John 3:11-24**

What is the relationship between loving God and loving people?

God doesn't have a physical body to embrace, or a hand to hold. So, how do we love God with our body?

Simple. We love others. We take all that we have learned through our mind combined with the passion that has kindled in our spirit, and we demonstrate God's love to the physical world.

We adopt the following attitude --

My stuff is not mine, but is a gift from God to be used for the greater good of everyone. I am not the center of the universe (God is) but am a contributing participant in this great family of humanity.

I reach out. I greet my neighbor and offer a genuine helping hand. I am aware of the sick, the poor, and the helpless and seek ways to fight for equity, assistance, healing, and reconciliation for those who cannot fend for themself. I look at those who are called my enemy and I seek ways to love them and bring peace. I look at the house my human family shares — the earth — and seek ways to preserve it and care for it, as God intended for us to do.

A Shift in Perspective

So far in this study we have discussed loving God in the language of personal relationship. It is you and God. Alone. Intimate. For a huge number of Christians in the Western, affluent culture, the idea of loving God has been sequestered or quarantined – or perhaps exiled – into the confines of a personal relationship with God. We have privatized our faith and made it all about *me*. In so doing, we have distorted Jesus' message of Good News into a selfish message in which *I* want to save *my* soul from an eternity in Hell by asking Jesus to come into *my* heart, to be *my personal savior*. Ironically, the phrase "invite Jesus to be your personal savior" is not found in the Bible.

Here's the harsh truth. You can't love God apart from loving people. Following Jesus is not a private, personal affair. Jesus did not come to save you as an isolated unit. He came to save the world, to save the dynamic of human civilization, so that the love of God permeates the very fabric of humanity. God created us in community, and the way of Jesus is the way that saves humanity from the Hell of isolation and self-centered individuation.

In order for those of us who are deeply influenced by the pervasive, affluent, individualistic, self-protective, and self-centered culture that has co-opted most of our spirituality, it will take some deep shifting of our paradigm to be able to reconnect the body to our mind and spirit in this pursuit of loving God with a whole heart.

Developing a Servant's Heart

> » **What does Paul command in Romans 12:1?**

> » **What comes to your mind when you hear the word servant?**

> » **Is the term *servant* a positive or a negative thing in your mind?**

» **What was Jesus' purpose in coming to this world? Mark 10:45**

» **Read John 13:1-17**

How did Jesus serve the disciples?

Why was Jesus able to give so freely of himself?

List several lessons you can learn from Christ's example in this passage.

» **Read Luke 9:46-48**

Who does Jesus consider to be "great"?

» **How should we be like Jesus? Philippians 2:5-8**

» **What perspective did Paul have on being a servant? 1 Corinthians 4:1-5**

» **How does having an attitude of humility affect how you relate to others? Philippians 2:3-4**

» **In your own words, what does it mean to be a servant of God? How should that look in your life?**

Your Stuff Belongs to God and others

God has given each one of us a special set of physical, practical, resources. These resources can be simply divided into three categories

▶ *Time: We all have 168 hours in a week.*
▶ *Talent: We all have unique skills and abilities – building, writing, art, singing, caring for children, cooking, computers, etc. – that God has given us.*
▶ *Treasure: God has given us each some level of income and financial standing.*

» **Read Matthew 25:14-30**

This is a parable that was designed to teach us a key principle about living in the Kingdom of God. In the parable the servants are given talents. In our day that would be around $1000 dollars per talent.

Read the story once through as it was written. Then read it a second time, only this time replace the word talent *with the phrase "time, talent, and treasure" and imagine that Jesus is the master and you are one of the servants.*

Were the talents distributed evenly? Why or why not?

What did the master expect the servants to do with the talents?

What were the rewards given to each servant?

Does this seem fair to you? Why or why not?

*God has given you a unique set of time, talents, and treasures.
How well are you using them for Him?*

» **Read Matthew 6:19-34**
   How should we view the stuff in our lives?

A Discipline of Giving

When God led Israel out of slavery He established the Law to help them learn how to be a nation and how to love God. In the Law God said, "Bring the best of the firstfruits of your soil to the house of the LORD your God." (Exodus 23:19 NIV) In those days almost everyone was a farmer, so the phrase "your soil" really meant "your income." The concept of firstfruits is simple: when God gives to us – whether it be in the form of time, talent, or treasure – we should give the firstfruits of the gift back to God. By doing this we demonstrate:

1. That we acknowledge that God is the giver of all things.
2. That we love God first above all things.
3. That we trust God will provide for our needs, even though we are giving out of the first and best of what we have received. This is a faith issue.

The big question is, "What do firstfruits look like in the 21st century? How much should we give?"

» **Read Leviticus 27:30 and Malachi 3:10**

How much did God expect his people to bring to him as an offering?

» **Now read 2 Corinthians 9:6-7**
How much did Paul say people should give when he was collecting for the poor?

Here's the bottom line. God has given you everything you have, both tangible and intangible. God is also interested in all that you are, both tangible and intangible. As followers of Jesus, one of the greatest ways that we can demonstrate our love for God with our body is to give to God out of the firstfruits of our time, talent, and treasure.

Spend some time evaluating how well you are giving to God and ask Him to show you how you could grow in this area.

Our Greatest Resource: Our Body

> » **Read 1 Corinthians 6:19-20**
> *How does God feel about our physical bodies?*

One of the greatest weaknesses in the American church today is the awareness of physical health. Please read the following excerpt from the book <u>What the Bible Says About Healthy Living</u> [1] by Dr. Rex Russell. M.D. and see if you might be interested in discovering what he has to say about taking care of the body God has given you.

"...a loving Creator has left us an instruction book that wonderfully matches the design of His creation... a large portion of the Scripture focuses on commands, ordinances and statutes that show us how to live on this carefully designed earth. Many of these passages pertain to subjects such as economics, law, government, interpersonal relationship, nutrition and health. The sacrifice of Jesus for our sins does not cancel the wisdom in these other teachings. As Paul said, they are still profitable (see 2 Tim. 3:16)

This book is not about miraculous intervention as an answer to prayer. Certainly God can do this in regard to illness when he chooses. This book is designed to help you discover the laws of God and apply them for health and wholeness. We will study other biblical and scientific laws that reveal how to recover and maintain health. You will see that the thoughts of our Creator are unparalleled in wisdom. You will experience firsthand what Florence Nightingale discovered: The laws of science are the thoughts of God."

(pp. 36-37)

[1] <u>What the Bible Says About Healthy Living</u> (Regal Books: Ventura, 2006)

> » Spend some time and ask yourself, "How well do my eating, sleeping, and exercising habits reflect my love and respect for the body that God has given me?"

> » How could you begin to love God with your body by cleaning up the temple a bit?

The Link

In the rest of this study we will explore Jesus' second command: Love your neighbor. In the overflow illustration this is shown as water spilling out into various "pots" of relational spheres in which we live. This illustration separates the two commands, as if it were possible to love God with a whole heart and not love your neighbor. It is not possible. Loving God with your body IS loving your neighbor.

There is a circular connection here, similar to the old question, "which came first, the chicken or the egg?" When Jesus spoke the command he said, "love your neighbor as yourself." If you don't love yourself, then you probably won't be able to love others very well. So, you need to focus on the truth that God loves you and see yourself as a cherished child of God. Then you will be able to love others as God loves them. On the other hand, as we have noted, you can't love God if you don't love others.

It boils down to a simple truth. As a follower of Jesus, we should not look at the world as a scary place and hope for the day that God takes us away and destroys all the "sinners" that scare us. Instead, we should realize that we are part of the physical creation that God loves and fully participate in it by loving everyone and everything, and seek to bring the peace of God to all nations. This is loving God with your body.

visit **www.vibbleblog.com/body** to find more resources regarding loving God with your BODY.

Group Discussion

» How do you feel about physical exercise: love it, hate it, love to hate it? Why?

» What is the relationship between the physical universe and the spiritual reality? How has this study either challenged or affirmed your view? Explain.

» Why is it important to develop a Servant's Heart?

» Summarize Jesus' teaching on material possessions. How do you respond to this?

» Do you think it is important to give? Why?

» What role does good physical health habits play in developing a love for God?

» What questions do you have from this week?

» What goals will you set to love God with your Body?

Session 5
Loving Your Comfortable Neighbor

Loving Others

Jesus boiled down all of the rules for living into two commands. He said we should love God and we should love our neighbor. So far in this study we have explored what it means to love God with our mind, spirit, and body. Jesus said that Loving God in this way is the first and primary commandment because He knew that if we truly abandon ourselves into the dynamic love relationship with God, then the second commandment will naturally spring forth as the overflow of our heart. If God's love is the center of our heart, then we will see everyone we meet through God's eyes and we will love them.

However, it is also important to focus on the second command, "to love your neighbor as yourself," because we sometimes have difficulty truly obeying the first commandment. Often we are more focused on self -- *my* pride, and *my* hurt – rather than on a relationship with God. Sometimes we don't feel the love of God, and in those moments we can look at other people and see them as different, or scary, or hinderances to *my* personal objectives.

Perhaps Jesus emphasized the second command because He knew that in learning to love others we will in turn learn new dimensions of God's love for us and will be able to love God more. There is a beautiful interplay between these two commands. The more I love God, the more I can love others, the more I love others the more I learn about God's love and can love God more deeply. This process is an upward spiral that develops within us a deeper and more intense capacity to love that will grow for all eternity.

Who is my neighbor?

Jesus' second command is to love your neighbor as yourself. The big question is, "Who is my neighbor?" In Luke 10 Jesus answered this question with the parable of the Good Samaritan. The ultimate answer is that EVERYONE is your neighbor, no matter who they are, and we are commanded to love them. For the purpose of this study, we will divide the term *neighbor* into two categories: **Comfortable Neighbors** and **Uncomfortable Neighbors**.

The comfortable neighbor can be further subdivided into the following categories:

> *Intimate Soul Mate* – if you are married, this is your spouse. If you are single, this is the person with whom you can be most open, transparent, and vulnerable.

> *Close Friends* – the average person has only 1-3 people in this category at any time. Jesus had Peter, James, and John – only 3 out of his 12 disciples.

> *Family* – depending upon your family of origin, this category may be closer to the center or further away from the center. Ideally, your family should be a safe place. Unfortunately this is often not the case.

> *Chosen Community* – this is the larger group of people with which we most identify. We know everyone's name, and we share enough common experience and/or values to feel "at home" with this group.

For the follower of Jesus, the Chosen Community category should be synonymous with the group of people we call our church. Everyone who follows Jesus is a part of the church or the Body of Christ that transcends political and ethnic boundaries. However, this universal church is very difficult to grasp and indentify with. The truth is that we, in a desire to find friends and a safe place, tend to flock together with people who are like-minded and share the same ethics and lifestyle. These gatherings are usually called churches.

Is it Really Necessary?

When we start to talk about community, some questions come to mind. Do we have to be in community? Where do we find community? What is community?

When we speak of community in our culture, it can take on different meanings. One sense of community is to think of living in a specific location, like Queens, NY, or North Las Vegas, NV. While that is a valid way of understanding the word, that is not the heart of what we are talking about. The better way to understand community, for this study, is to speak of it in terms of *intentional relationship*. To be in community is to be involved in people's lives in a more-than-surface relationship where you intend to know them and be known by them at an intimate level.

Is this kind of community necessary for a healthy and balanced spiritual life? Absolutely. That question is like asking whether it is necessary for a human being to eat food and drink water. Are eating and drinking optional? Yes, but you won't get to make that choice for long because you won't survive.

Created for Community

Being involved in community is part of the DNA of what it means to be human. God created us for the purpose of fellowship with the Divine Triune Community. God is three persons in one essence. Think of it this way; God IS a loving community. The three persons of the Godhead eternally love one another. God (the loving community) created us in God's image -- male and female. We were not created as individuals in God's image, we were created as community in God's image; male and female living in perfect unity.

When sin and the knowledge of evil entered the picture, all lines of fellowship were severed and the very image of God was disrupted within us. Not only is it important for us to be in a spiritual community, it is vital to our spiritual transformation because it was for community that we were created.

Body Life

The Bible gives us many helpful analogies that paint a picture of what it means to be in a Christ community. We are the bride of Christ, the flock, the branches, and the temple. One image that is very helpful to understand how we can live in community is that of the body.

» **Read**

Romans 12:3-8
What should our attitude be towards other members of the body?

1 Corinthians 12:12-27
What holds the body together as one unit?

Ephesians 4:1-16
What brings unity to the body? What is the ultimate goal of the body? What will the body look like when we get to that point?

Where everybody knows your name

In the 1980's and 90's one of the most popular shows on television was *Cheers*. Week after week millions of Americans peeked into the lives of a handful of misfits that found their common meeting ground in a little downstairs bar in Boston. Why did we love that show so much? Part of it was the well written comic banter between the characters, there is no doubt. But, another reason we loved it so much is found in the lyrics of the show's theme song. "You want to go where everybody knows your name." In our culture we encounter the faceless crowds every day. We are constantly confronted with hostile strangers and corporate greed that threatens to suck the joy of life right from our bones. We long for one person who really knows us and cares about us. Sadly, many of us turn to fictitious characters -- either on TV or in books -- to somehow fill this void in our lives. Somehow we feel connected to these characters more than we do to real people. Why is this? Perhaps what draws us to these stories is the interconnectedness of the characters. Even though they are not perfect, the characters in those stories know each other intimately and, through thick and thin, better or worse, continue to meet together and stick up for each other. Bottom line, we all want to find a place where everybody knows our name and cares about us for who we are.

Unfortunately, most Americans have to settle for artificial friendship created through television shows or through cyberspace. As Americans we are sent conflicting signals. On the one hand we uphold friendships like the ones in the T.V. shows, but on the other hand we are told that we need to look out for number one (me) and try to get ahead in life, no matter the cost. Those two values don't work well together. It doesn't have to be like that. Let's look at what the community of Christ is supposed to look like and how we can truly be in a place where we are known and know others on a real and intimate level.

» **Read Acts 2:42-47**

To what were the people devoted? Why?

How would you describe the general spirit or attitude of the community?

Where did they meet?

There are many ways that we would like to emulate this first church in Jerusalem. For right now let's focus on where they met. Remember that at the beginning of Acts 2 it says that 3,000 people were added to the church on the first day of its existence, and then it kept growing. This was no small gathering of people. How could such a large group of people function as an intimate community? The key to their community was the fact that they met in two places, they met in the temple courts and in their homes.

The temple courts

In Jerusalem the temple court (also known as Solomon's Porch) was the common meeting place for any teacher and his followers. Jesus met in the temple courts to teach the people whenever he visited the city. All the prominent rabbis would gather and teach here. It was also the place where the local news and information was shared with the city. It was the common forum for the culture. It only makes sense that the church would gather together in a large group in the place where large groups naturally gather in order to hear the teachings about their Lord and Saviour Jesus Christ.

In their homes

Here lies the secret to the success of this church. Look at what the people did in their homes, "They broke bread in their homes and ate together with glad and sincere hearts, praising God and enjoying the favor of all the people." In other words they were able to be human beings together in their homes. Just think about the logistics of this for a minute. With 3,000+ people in one church, how could they possibly care for each other and be the body of Christ? How could they even know everyone's name? But when they met in homes they had to limit the numbers to the amount of people that could fit around the table and have dinner together. In that intimate setting, with food in their hands, they could take the time to get to know people at a deeper level. In their homes they shared communion, ate meals, prayed, enjoyed each other's company, and enjoyed the favor of all the people.

If your involvement in a local church is going to cultivate your soul and create a space where you can grow in loving your neighbor, then it will have to grow beyond filling a seat on Sunday morning. Corporate Worship services are nice. They fill a need, much like the gathering in the Temple Court. However, you are merely a spectator there, a nameless face in a crowd; especially if the congregation is larger than 100 people.

Depending upon the infrastructure of your church, there are many ways to get involved in a smaller group where you can begin to cultivate closer relationships with people in your safe community. Some methods that churches use are: small groups, house churches, cell groups, task cells, Adult Bible Fellowship, Bible Studies, special interest groups. For the purpose of this study, we will use the term "small group" to refer to any intentional group that moves you out of the large crowd and into meaningful relationships.

A Place where we can BELONG.

Belong to
   each other

Encourage
   each other
   to Grow

Link through
   ccountability

One Another...

Needs Met
   through
   Spiritual
   Gifts

Give Light
   to the World

In the following study we will explore what a small group should look like. Think of each of these points as a contrast between what you CAN do in a small group that you COULD NEVER do in a large group. In a small group you can **B.E.L.O.N.G.**

Belong to each other

> » **Read Romans 12:5**
> *How are the parts related to each other?*

One way to think of the word *belong* is that we *long to be* with each other. In a small group you can make friends and personal connections that bond you to other people.

Do you remember in the show Cheers what would happen when the one character who sat on the corner stool would walk into the bar? Everyone would yell, "Norm!" What a great feeling! Isn't that what we want - a place where everyone would greet us by name? When you walk into a large crowd that doesn't happen. If you are an average person you walk into a large crowd and simply become one nameless face in a sea of strangers.

However, in a small group when you walk in, they shout your name because they actually know who you are. They give you a hug, you have a cup of coffee together, and they ask you how your week was. It is wonderful! In a small group you can long to be with specific people who love you and long to be with you.

Encourage each other to grow.

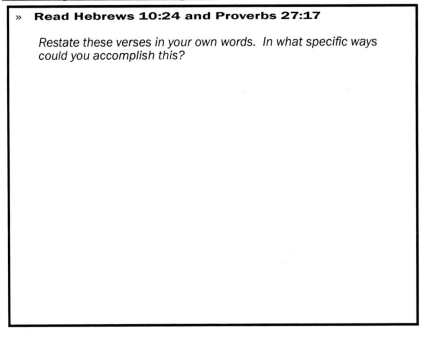

» **Read Hebrews 10:24 and Proverbs 27:17**

Restate these verses in your own words. In what specific ways could you accomplish this?

We could call this the spiritual buddy system. Think of a time when you were involved in a sport or a competive talent like playing the piano. You probably had a partner or a trainer that pushed you when you felt like giving up. The same is true in our spiritual lives. Let's face it, living according to Jesus' plan of living is not easy. Living for ourselves and taking the smooth road would be a lot more comfortable. We need each other to get in each other's faces and remind ourselves why we are taking the road less traveled.

Link through accountability

> » **Read Galatians 6:1-2**
>
> *What are we called to do? What is the warning? How can you be involved without getting tripped up?*

Imagine that you were attending a church where your only experience was to attend a service with hundreds of other people. If you were there would you lean over to the stranger next to you and say, "Listen, I've really been struggling with lust, and there is this one Internet site that I've been trying to stay away from. I was wondering if you would pray for me and ask me next week how I did"? YEAH, RIGHT! You would never talk like that to the people you meet at a big service. At Big Church we put on our happy Christian face and say, "How's it going?" "Great! How are you doing?" "Great!" "Good to hear it." "See you next week." Then we go home to our loneliness, our sin, and our isolation.

In a small group you can get to the heart of the matter. The sad truth is that each one of us, at one time or another, carries a specific burden of sin that weighs us down and holds us prisoner. We are convinced that we are the only one who struggles with this sin and would be mortified if anyone knew about it. In a small group you have the opportunity to be in a safe place where people will listen to your pain and shortcomings and will lovingly support you. You'll be relieved to know that you aren't the only one struggling with sin and that someone else can truly relate to your situation. In the small group we can hold each other accountable to overcome the sin or blind spots in our lives and get on with the business of godly living.

One another one another

No, that wasn't a typo. In the New Testament there are many verses that command us to "one another." (i.e. love one another, forgive one another, etc.) In a small group you can "one another one another." Once again, fulfilling these commands would be impossible if our Christian experience existed completely in a large group context.

» **Read the following verses and write down what we are to do to/for one another. Next to that write down a specific example of how this could be acted out in your life.**

Galatians 5:13

Romans 15:7

Colossians 3:13

Romans 16:16

Galatians 6:2

Romans 12:10

Romans 15:14

Ephesians 5:21

1 Thessalonians 5:11

Needs are met through exercising spiritual gifts

» **Read 1 Peter 4:10**

*What are we supposed to use in order to serve one another?
What does this mean?*

As we have mentioned already, the Bible often refers to the church as a body. In the human body each part has a specific function and contribution to the body. The small group is the ideal place to discover and exercise the role that God has given you to play in the body. In the small group the encouragers get to encourage, the helpers get to help, the leaders get to lead, the teachers get to teach, the administrators get to organize, and on the list goes on. The small group creates an environment in which every member of the community has the opportunity to explore and exercise his or her spiritual gifts in a way that a large group setting could never offer.

Give light to the world

> » **Read John 17:20-23**
>
> *What was Jesus' prayer for us? Why did He want this for us? How well do you think the church is doing in this area?*

The world can't see the physical Jesus anymore. He was only here for 33 short years. So, how can they know him? They can still see his body on earth...it's called the church. We are the only Jesus that the world will see. How we love each other and get along with each other is the loudest and strongest testimony to the truth of Jesus that exists. It is sad to say that the church throughout history has not done a very good job of obeying Jesus in the area of unity. Christians tend to shoot each other over secondary issues quite a bit.

While the large group church may struggle with unity, the small group has the potential to overcome this weakness. In a small group we have the opportunity to actually work through our differences and carry out constructive conflict resolution. We can realize what it truly means to fulfill Paul's words in Ephesians 4:15 and speak the truth in love. We can love someone and be in unity in the midst of diversity. When that kind of thing happens in small groups all across the country, then the light of Jesus will begin to shine brightly. We can tell our friends and neighbors, "Hey, I've found a place where people actually love each other selflessly. It's not just a superficial niceness; this can only be a supernatural love." When that happens and Jesus is exalted in our unity then people will be authentically drawn to him in repentance and reconciliation.

*visit **www.vibbleblog.com/neighbor** to find more resources regarding loving your NEIGHBOR.*

Group Discussion

» **Tell about a time when you had a good friend. What made it special?**

» **Is it important to develop close relationships with people who believe the same way you do? Why?**

» **What are the benefits of a "small group" as opposed to the "large group"? How have you seen this to be true in your own experience?**

» **When you look at the different aspects of BELONG, which of those things seems most attractive or needed for your life right now? Why?**

» **After just a few weeks of meeting together, in what ways is your study group fulfilling some of the BELONG statements?**

» **What goals could your group set that will help you to grow in one of the BELONG statements?**

Session 6
Loving Your Larger Neighborhood

It's all about Love

In this session we come to the final section of our overflow chart. Jesus commanded us to simply love God and love our neighbor. We've talked about loving God with our mind, spirit, and body so that we can be filled with his love to the point of overflowing his love to others. Last week we divided up the idea of neighbor into two sections: the Comfortable Neighbor who is in our intimate community, and the Uncomfortable Neighbor who is different than us.

It is one thing to love a person in your church who shares a common value system and speaks the same "God speak" that you do. But, to love someone who is very different than you, or, worse yet, antagonistic toward you, is another matter. Today we must ask the really difficult question...

Who is my neighbor?

» **Read Luke 10:25-37**

In order to understand this story you must be aware that there was extreme prejudice between the Jews in Jerusalem and the people who lived in Samaria (Samaritans). The Jews felt that the Samaritans were dogs and not worthy of God's Love or His Kingdom.

In light of this prejudice, what is the irony in Jesus' parable?

The question asked to Jesus was, "who is my neighbor?" Put Jesus' answer to that question into your own words.

You've got the cure!

In our society today there are few things more horrific than the reality of diseases like cancer and AIDS that are killing thousands upon thousands of people. Very few of us have escaped the pain of losing someone close to us to one of these diseases. Modern medicine has struggled for decades to try to break the code to these killers, and yet people continue to die.

Imagine how incredible it would be if you found the cure to one of these killers. Picture it, right now, you hold in your hands the undeniable, guaranteed cure for AIDS. What would you do with it? Would you stuff it in your sock drawer and hope no one saw you with it? Would you only talk about it to the other scientists who invented it? Perhaps you would form a club for those inventors where you would meet together and discuss how neat it would be if everyone knew about this cure.

NO WAY!! You would rush out into the street and start shouting to the people that you've found the cure. You'd call all the news stations and magazines. You'd put up a web page. You'd place an ad in all the papers advertising that the pain and suffering is over.

There is a much worse disease in the world than AIDS. In fact, this disease makes AIDS look like the common cold. Traditionally it has been called "sin". We are all infected. The symptoms are selfishness, hardness around the heart, a sense of being alone. The prognosis? Not good. When we are operating contrary to the way of God's love, it creates dis-unity, dis-chord, and dis-ease. It leads to fear, which leads to hatred, which leads to war, which leads to poverty, starvation, sickness, and death. Pretty grim isn't it? I can hear the moaning and the agony of the infected crying out in the streets right now. Can you hear them? They are lost and dying and in need of a cure.

But wait. You have one. Right now, in your hands, in your heart, you have the cure for sin. Jesus' message is the cure. He showed us the way of God's love. He spoke it with his words, he lived it with his actions, he demonstrated it with his death, he empowered it with his resurrection. Jesus said in John 11:25-26 (NIV),

> **I am the resurrection and the life. He who believes in me will live, even though he dies; and whoever lives and believes in me will never die.**

The undeniable, guaranteed cure for sin and death has been created and is readily available to the world.

The question that remains for you is, "What are you going to do with it? Are you going to stuff it in your sock drawer? Are you going to go to church and talk about it with those who have already found it and imagine how wonderful it would be if other people found this cure?

NO WAY!! The Apostle Paul said in Romans 10:14-15 (NIV),

> How, then, can they call on the one they have not believed in? And how can they believe in the one of whom they have not heard? And how can they hear without someone preaching to them? And how can they preach unless they are sent? As it is written, "How beautiful are the feet of those who bring good news!"

Biblical mandate

» **In Matthew 28:18-20, what does Jesus command his disciples to do?**

» **In Acts 1:8, what did Jesus promise to give his disciples? Why? Where did he tell them to go? Why?**

» **What is the Gospel as stated in 1 Corinthians 15:1-4 (NIV)**

» **What attitudes did Paul have about sharing the Gospel?**

Acts 20:24

Romans 1:15-16

Loving Jerusalem

There is a simple, yet profound, truth in Acts 1:8. Jesus told the disciples to go to Jerusalem, Judea and Samaria, and to the ends of the earth. We can think of these three categories as spheres of safety. The first sphere is the safest sphere. It is that group of people that are naturally in our own personal sphere of influence; our friends, family, and co-workers. The first sphere is our JERUSALEM. The second sphere is the group or groups of people who are not in our natural and comfortable relational sphere, but share the same local geographical sphere. In other words, these are the people who live in our city but are from other cultural and/or socio-economic strata than us. This sphere is our SAMARIA. The third sphere is pretty much everyone else in the world that has not yet heard the good news of Jesus. This is the ENDS OF THE EARTH.

Loving your Jerusalem is simple. It doesn't take great skill or years of training. It simply takes two things.

1. Authentically love God and be filled with His love as a daily discipline. Remember, it's all about overflow.
2. Be courageous enough to be authentically in love with God in front of everyone you interact with, regardless of who they are.

If you are being transformed by the Spirit then the people in your Jerusalem will notice. As they do, then be prepared to simply tell them what Jesus has done for you. Invite them to church. Love them unconditionally. Be ready to lead them into the same relationship that you have with Jesus.

> » **On the opposite page, make a relationship map of your Jerusalem. Write down the names of all the people who are in your natural sphere of influence. Spend some time asking God to show you how to be intentional about sharing your faith with these people.**

Your Jerusalem

Loving Samaria

It is time that we move out of the comfortable region of Jerusalem and begin to cross the borders into Samaria and beyond.

Stop! Before we can move into Samaria we need to get something very clear. Over the last several decades a dangerous concept has crept into the average American Evangelical church. We have come to believe that the "good news" of Jesus, and the process of "salvation" is simply to speak words to people about Jesus and lead them to pray the "sinner's prayer." If we have done that, then we have adequately "evangelized the lost" and done our part. If a person rejects our words, then their doom is on their own head.

Here's the problem. The good news of Jesus is not merely words. It is not a trite slogan or a catchy sales pitch. The good news of Jesus is a way of life. If we are going to effectively understand our Samaria and know how to reach the ends of the Earth then we need to understand what the Kingdom of God really looks like and what we have been truly called to do in the world.

True Religion

» **Read James 1:26-27. What is true religion?**

» **Read Isaiah 58:3-10**

In vv. 3-5, what accusation does the Lord bring against His people? Why?

In vv. 6-7, what picture does the Lord paint of what his people should be doing?

In vv. 8-10, what will be the result of living according to God's plan?

» **What is God's attitude toward the poor in Deuteronomy 15:7-15? What are His instructions concerning the poor?**

» **Read the following Proverbs and list their instructions and advice regarding the poor.**

Proverbs 3:27-28

Proverbs 11:25

Proverbs 22:9

Proverbs 25:21

Proverbs 28:27

» **Read Matthew 25:34-40. What did the sheep do that granted them entrance into the inheritance?**

» **In 1 Corinthians 13:3. Does "doing good for the poor" make you a "good" person? Why or why not?**

» **Read 1 John 3:16-20. According to these verses, what does love look like?**

» **According to this study, what does Loving Your World really look like?**

Loving Samaria - cont'd

Peter and Cornelius

» **Read Acts 10.**

How did the Jews feel about the Romans?

What was Peter's reaction to being called to the home of a Roman centurion?

What lesson did Peter learn from this experience? In what way was he challenged?

A Survey of Samaria

> » **Read Matthew 5:13-16. What are we called to be?**

Think about your city. Within a 50 mile radius of where you live, how many cultures and races are represented?

Also, within a 50 mile radius of your home, how many people are poor and homeless? How many of them are being abused or oppressed by crime and substance abuse? How many of them feel that there is no way out of their circumstances? How well are we shining the light of Jesus' good news to them? Are we a light set on a hill that cannot be hidden or are we hiding our light under the bushel of our safe little small groups?

The following is a list of the kinds of circumstances that place people in the desperate need of a helping hand. Take some time to read the list and ponder each one. Ask God to help you add to this list more circumstances that you have encountered. Ask God to show you ways that you could be a part of reaching these hurting people with true religion.

- ▶ *Homeless*
- ▶ *AIDS patients*
- ▶ *Battered women*
- ▶ *Women with unwanted pregnancy and children in danger of being aborted*
- ▶ *Poor children*
- ▶ *Prisoners*
- ▶ *Drug addicts*
- ▶ *Immigrants who are just getting started and battling against prejudice*
- ▶ *Illiterate*

Loving the Whole world

You may be thinking to yourself, "How can I possibly reach the whole world?" Well...you can't. Alone, you can't really make much of a difference. However, you were not designed to be alone, nor were you called to work alone. One of the greatest lessons we can learn as we try to grasp loving the whole world is to realize that we are part of something much bigger than our local church. Too many times we think that our local church or specific denomination is the only real church. That just isn't true. The truth is that there is only one church and all the denominations are pieces of it..

» **Read Ephesians 4:1-6**

How should we view our relationship with others?

God is at work all over the world in ways that you could never dream of. We are part of the universal body of Christ. We are each one small part, but if every small part does what it has been asked to do, then the mission of the body will be accomplished.

When discussing the topic of reaching the entire world with the good news of Jesus it is important to keep one thing in mind: that "other" place is just like your Samaria...just further away. In other words, people are people and they share the same basic needs no matter where they live. There are hungry, poor, addicted, battered, illiterate, and oppressed people in every area of the world. And we all need Jesus.

There are three ways that a person can be involved in the global arena of loving the World.

1. We can use our financial resources to support missionaries and world relief organizations. America is the richest country in the world. We are 20% of the world's population, but we consume 80% of the world's resources. It is our obligation to use our resources to help the people in countries that have absolutely nothing. As an individual and as a church we need to be praying about how we can increase our financial support of organizations that are out on the frontlines making a difference in these areas.

2. God may be calling you to actually go somewhere. Perhaps the part that you are called to play in your local church is be a global extension of who it is. Maybe it can support you to fulfill your calling in a place like Sudan or Venezuela, or Indonesia. Be willing to hear the call if God is making it. The call is not for everyone, but if it is for you, then be sure not to turn a deaf ear.

3. Become educated and concerned about our country's political and philosophical system that breeds selfishness, self-indulgence, social class segregation, self-preservation, exploitation of weaker people groups, and unhealthy consumption of natural resources. Find ways to bring change, and the way of Jesus, to these systems.

The Home we Share

In the Westernized version of the Gospel, especially among the evangelical traditions, there has been a tendency to ignore one huge piece of what it means to be in God's Kingdom -- the planet. God created us to be stewards and caretakers of the earth. The planet, and all its natural resources, are not here for our selfish consumption, they are God's creation and loved by God as much as we are. God has entrusted us to take good care of this place, and in so doing, we will maintain a healthy and safe place for the generations of people that will follow us.

Unfortunately, certain theological perspectives have come to develop an attitude that says, "We're heading toward the end times, and God is going to destroy this place, anyway, isn't he? So, why shouldn't we get what we can out of it while there's still time." This escapist and annihilationist theology is dangerous and can have very counter-kingdom effects on both our souls and the planet if we don't put it in check and find a better way.

The way of Jesus is the way of other-oriented love. It is a place where we stop and ask, "is what I am about to say and do the best decision for EVERYONE, or is it something that will bring short term gain to only a small group of people at the expense of others?" A truly holistic spirituality that is centered on the way of Jesus should encompass a global, environmentally conscious awareness and ethic that empowers nations to work together to find ways to preserve our natural resources and find creative and life-giving ways to provide for the needs of everyone on the planet.

Resources

Here is a very small sampling of organizations and opportunities that exist in which you can be involved. Ask God to show you how you can be involved. Also ask God to show you additional opportunities that can be added to the list.

Donate:
► *Prison Fellowship (evangelism and discipleship of US prisoners) www.prisonfellowship.org*
► *Bread for the World (grassroots advocacy network on domestic and international hunger issues) www.bread.org*
► *World Vision (relief and development organization) http://www.worldvision.org*
► *Compassion International (child sponsorship program) www.compassion.com*
► *Voice of the Martyrs (advocacy, awareness and care for persecuted and imprisoned Christians) www.persecution.com*
► *Habitat for Humanity (home building for homeless and needy families) www.habitat.org*

Petition signing, letter writing and advocacy:
► *DATA ("Debt, AIDS, Trade, Africa" Advocacy group for African suffering) http://www.data.org/*

► *World Vision (relief and development organization) http://www.worldvision.org/*

► *Oxfam (fights global poverty, hunger and injustice) www.oxfamamerica.org*

► *Voice of the Martyrs (advocacy, awareness and care for persecuted and imprisoned Christians) www.persecution.com*

Volunteer work:
► *Habitat for Humanity (home building for homeless and needy families) www.habitat.org*
► *Amor Ministries (Mexico mission trips) http://www.amor.org/*
► *Second Harvest (food bank organization) http://www.secondharvest.org/*
► *STEM (short term global missions) http://www.stemmin.org/*

visit **www.vibbleblog.com/neighbor** *to find more resources regarding loving your NEIGHBOR.*

Group Discussion

» Tell about a time when you encountered a person or a group of people that made you feel very uncomfortable. Why do you think it felt that way?

» According to Jesus, who is our neighbor? How do you respond to this idea?

» How did you react to the idea that the world is sick and you know the cure? Why?

» What does it mean to "make disciples of all nations"?

» Jesus said to "teach them to obey all that I have instructed." What two commands did he give? What difference might it make in the world if everyone obeyed Jesus' two commands?

» What does your "Samaria" look like?

» Do you think that being actively involved in social justice issues and environmental issues is a valid part sharing the Gospel? Why?

» How will you get involved in loving your uncomfortable neighbor?

Session 7
Conclusion

A Path of Disciplined Grace

Throughout this study we've talked about practical things that you can do to help you grow spiritually. We've investigated what it means to develop a Divine Romance with God and receive God's love through our Mind, Spirit, and Body. We've explored what it means to love your neighbor as yourself. We've seen the importance of being in a spiritual community. We've also seen how important it is that we look at the larger community and be involved in the global family of humanity.

After looking at all of these issues you might be overwhelmed by a laundry list of spiritual to-dos and think, "I'll never be a good person!"

Take a deep breath.

Remember, it's not about doing something in order to earn God's love. It's about training yourself to become more able to grow. Go back to the picture of the Vine. Jesus didn't say, "Go produce fruit!" He said, "Remain in me." Abide. Dwell. Breathe in, breathe out.

We don't do things in order to earn God's favor or change the world. We do things that will create space within our lives for God to do the miraculous work of transformation in us and through us. We fill, then we overflow.

Read the following passage from one of the classic books on spiritual formation titled <u>The Celebration of Discipline</u> by Richard Foster. Ask God to speak to you about this subject.

...it would be proper to speak of "the path of disciplined grace." It is "grace" because it is free; "disciplined" because there is something for us to do. In The Cost of Discipleship Dietrich Bonhoeffer makes it clear that grace is free, but it is not cheap. The grace of God is unearned and unearnable, but if we ever expect to grow in grace, we must pay the price of a consciously chosen course of action which involves both individual and group life. Spiritual growth is the purpose of the Disciplines.

It might be helpful to visualize what we have been discussing. Picture a long, narrow ridge with a sheer drop-off on either side. The chasm to the right is the way of moral bankruptcy through human strivings for righteousness. Historically this has been called the heresy of moralism. The chasm to the left is moral bankruptcy through the absence of human strivings. This has been called the heresy of antinomianism. On the ridge there is a path, the Disciplines of the spiritual life. This path leads to the inner transformation and healing for which we seek. We must never veer off to the right or the left, but stay on the path. The path is fraught with severe difficulties, but also with incredible joys. As we travel on this path, the blessing of God will come upon us and reconstruct us into the image of Jesus Christ. We must always remember that the path does not produce the change; it only places us where the change can occur. This is the path of disciplined grace. [1]

[1] Celebration of Discipline (HarperCollins: New York, 1998)

Setting Spiritual Goals

It's time to review. Spend time looking over the past sessions of study. Ask God to show you one way that you could grow in each of these areas over the course of the next year.

Be prepared to share these goals with your group on Sunday.

▶ *To better love God with my MIND, I plan to...*

▶ *To better love God with my SPIRIT, I plan to...*

▶ *To better love God with my BODY, I plan to...*

▶ **To better overflow God's love to my COMFORTABLE COMMUNITY, I plan to...**

► *To better overflow God's love to my*
UNCOMFORTABLE COMMUNITY, I plan to...

Group Discussion

» **Think about the thoughts and feelings you had about joining this study group before it started. In what ways have they changed now that you are finished?**

» **Share your response to Richard Foster's comments.**

» **Share some of the goals that you have set in the five areas of the Overflow Principle.**

» **Discuss ways that the group members can help each other stick with these goals.**

» **Make plans for the next step of this group's life. Will you:**

  ▶ *Disband*

  ▶ *Continue meeting with the same group of people*

  ▶ *Continue meeting and invite new people*

  ▶ *What will you study?**

  ▶ *Who and how will you invite new people?*

*a suggested next study is ***The Life of Jesus***. This is a 15-week study that leads the group through all four Gospels and a complete overview of Jesus' life and teachings. It is available at *www.vibblebooks.com*

A Suggested Model for Running this Small Group Study

▶ Set a regularly scheduled meeting time, once a week, and stick to it.

▶ Set the expectation that everyone will come to the meeting having done the study during the week and prepared to participate in the discussion.

▶ Designate a facilitator of the group who will be empowered to call the group back on task and keep the discussion focused on the goals of the lesson. This may be the same person for each meeting, or the role may rotate from meeting to meeting. Either way, acknowledge who is the facilitator before the discussion begins, then let that person facilitate!

▶ Set aside 1 hour and 30 minutes for your weekly meeting.

▶ Always have food! Meeting for a meal is ideal, but if you can't do a meal, at least have some sort of refreshments to eat. Meeting and eating creates a much more casual and intimate setting for authentic conversation.

▶ Here are two suggested meeting schedules:
  ◊ **Option A: The Meal Meeting**
  - 30 min: share a meal, allow the conversation to wander
  - 45 min: allow each person an opportunity to share their answers to the group discussion questions.
  - 15 min: pray for one another. Either share requests verbally to each other and God, or break up into groups of two or three and pray for one another.
  - end on time! People with child care needs will value this.
  ◊ **Option B: The Snack Meeting**
  - 15 min: small-talk, mingling, share about the week
  - 45 min: allow each person an opportunity to share their answers to the group discussion questions.
  - 15 min: pray for one another. Either share requests verbally to each other and God, or break up into groups of two or three and pray for one another.
  - 15 min: dig into the snacks and let the conversation happen.
  - end on time! People with child care needs will value this.

▶ Make an effort to connect with your group members outside of the group meeting: a phone call, email, coffee meeting, etc.

▶ Have fun, stay flexible, and expect that God will do great things in and through the space that you have created with the group.

About the Author

Steve Thomason is first and foremost a child of God that is committed to loving his wife and four children. He currently resides in the suburbs of Minneapolis, Minnesota.

Steve has two passions in life. The first is teaching people about God and how to grow in a relationship with the Creator. His second passion is art -- specifically cartooning and animation. Throughout his career he has sought to blend these two passions together to create visually interesting lessons that draw people closer to God.

From 1994-2002 Steve was in Adult Minstries at Central Christian Church in Las Vegas, Nevada. During those years Steve led small group ministries, adult education classes, and wrote curriculum for both settings. Along the way he earned a Masters of Divinity degree from Bethel Theological Seminary through their In-Ministry Program.

In 2002 Steve and his family joined with a group of friends to explore what it would look like to "do church" in a different way. For the next 5 years they experimented with being a community in a network of house churches called Hart Haus. During those years Steve wrote a daily Bible Study that combined cartoons and Bible Commentary.

In 2009 Steve set out on a new leg of his teacher/artist journey. He took the Hart Haus studies and used them as the foundation for creating Vibble Books. His desire is to see Vibble Books and VibbleSpace.com become a resource for his generation to engage with the reality of God's Love so that God's Kingdom can be realized in our world.

More titles from Vibble Books

The Life of Jesus

a 15-week, 5-day per week study that will guide you through all four Gospels, woven together in a chronological presentation of Jesus' life.

Acts

a 12-week, 5-day per week study that will guide you through the book of Acts. This is the story of the first generation of Jesus-folowers as they spread from Jerusalem throughout the Roman Empire.

Paul's Letters

a 16-week, 5-day per week guide through all of the letters that Paul wrote both to churches and individuals. Through these letters we have a model of how to contextualize Jesus' message for specific cultural issues.

View all the titles at www.vibblebooks.com

The learning adventure doesn't stop with the printed studies. Visit www.VibbleSpace.com and witness the Vibble in its natural habitat. At VibbleSpace.com you can watch teaching animations and interact with others who are using Vibble Books material.

Workshops and Seminars

Steve is available to provide workshops and seminars for your church as a suplemental resource to the group studies.

Contact him at info@vibblebooks.com to learn more.

Printed in the United States
218426BV00002B/1/P